# Hover

# Hover

**Erin Malone**

TEBOT BACH • HUNTINGTON BEACH • CALIFORNIA • 2015

Hover
Copyright © 2015 by Erin Malone

The Patricia Bibby First Book Prize, 2013
Judge, Ralph Angel

Design and layout: Michael Wada
Cover Art: Risen, by Eric Zener, www.ericzener.com
Author Photo: David Delfs

ISBN 10: 1-939678-13-7
ISBN 13: 978-1-939678-13-3

Library of Congress Control Number: 2014956689

1st Edition

A Tebot Bach book

Tebot Bach, Welsh for little teapot, is A Nonprofit Public Benefit
Corporation, which sponsors workshops, forums, lectures, and
publications. Tebot Bach books are distributed by Small Press
Distribution, Armadillo and Ingram.

The Tebot Bach Mission: Advancing Literacy,
Strengthening Community, and transforming life
experiences with the power of poetry through readings,
workshops, and publications.

This book is made possible through a grant from The
San Diego Foundation Steven R. and Lera B. Smith Fund
at the recommendation of Lera Smith.

www.tebotbach.org

*For Shawn & Peter,*
*and in memory of Michael Malone (1972-1983)*

# Contents

## Symbols to Guide Your Viewing (III)

*Hover*

Erin Malone


Every reality is a given. A husband. A son. A life on the East coast, and then in the West. And yet, at the same time, "Reality exists," wrote George Orwell, "in the human mind, and nowhere else." A kid brother, a soul mate who died when we were what, 11 or 12 years old? A word we no longer have for it. For reality, that is.

There are certain kinds of loss that alter consciousness forever, because that which is gone never goes away. There is a kind of sadness that, after a while, slips into madness. The son or the brother. The husband, from that far away.

"If she could rest / she'd tilt her chair to watch / holes in the overturned bowl of her skull," Erin Malone writes. All around and through the orderly, finely-crafted poems in Erin Malone's most impressive first book, *Hover*, reality exists—as in blurred, as in upset, as in sorrow, as in prayer. Reality, after all, is all about courage.

Ralph Angel

*A body is a place missed specifically.*

—Brenda Hillman

# Symbols to Guide Your Viewing  (I)

**Straight or meandering lines:**
uncooked spaghetti on the floor;
winter rain pecking the windows;
traveling tracks of one who must
forage and return; also, cooked
spaghetti hanging from the child's
mouth; an unfinished thought—; all
my sentences

## >>:
pair of boomerangs; tits like socks on
the shower bar; or a bend in the
river; pinched mouths; stinging
words; steady wind; skating on thin
ice; nevertheless our knees point
forward.

## Suspect

Curtains float
& the house

docks, all its clocks

poker-faced & blank. Dishes:
done. The day's

animal is down.
        The house settles

but the night, let in, listens

like a guilty twin
to my out-loud wandering.

Lately a line drawing,
I live in air—

Where's my fill, my plush

other, illustrated life?
That I tired of

& traded, willingly
        it seems & still

I would,
I cannot solve it, yet now, now

I miss my love

        am ruined by the loss

of mouth & tongue/ *his*
mouth/ *his*

tongue/ & my
      wants

washed &
folded away! My-

self, aproned, pocketed!

     Mind,
          what have we done?

Tell me where the body is.

     The moon's small

mercury clings
to the handle & drain.

## Directions

Stranger, I can't smile right.
One whole side of my face
is sliding. A hillside, this body

isn't what I thought. Like a foreign country
it demands instructions: *Lay out and identify*

*all parts.* Who am I to drive
its unknown, ingrown roads? The waxy
poppies closed against orange

parking lights, all the blind curves. My map
won't fold and I need even simple things
spelled out, the words

for house, the room that means
a kitchen. *Unwrap before cooking.*
*Cook before eating.* Until now I've avoided

eye contact but like the flowers
my flame is low. Please will you offer

your assistance? Here I don't know how to say
my name, but am learning to read
the smallest gestures.

## Mornings,

when I descended
everything had been done for me—eggs on toast, toast
on plates—The baby's nose

too large for his face. I held him like a present

while a woman with pins in her mouth
hemmed my dress to the floor.

## Wearing the Terrarium

My head is a guest, a Gulliver
parting the dirt, eyes at the earthworms
then up. Firs around my shoulders.

When I walk I carry the scene.
Cubed, the sky is itself but groomed
to change more slowly. Exhale of clouds:

I balance the books
and straighten and still. The thud
in my ears is a big bass drum

I shout! To hear myself think.
I stuck my head in a house.
Something turned over.

## Lament for Seven Minus Some

If one pound gone, then where?
To the folds of his blanket,
the sails of his out-bound cries?
A shred, a hair's-
          breadth, *a small, small loss.*

I find moths, flies'
asterisks on the sills
& sweep them out with October's leaves.

Above the eaves, a thin-lipped moon.

(One-tenth of his body's weight
          is whose fault but my body's?)

*Normal for a newborn,* this vanishing.
A spare minute, too-light print
on rice paper, end of a sentence
I forget. A pinch, a peck,
          the sock that's slipping off—

My imagination
          curls.

## Objects Not Visible to the Human Eye

I wear the house like a box, turning inside
when one wall looks worn. If I go out,
it's just to the market or bank, where
they compliment the baby for the fringe

around his eyes. *Who does he look like?*
I've stopped checking mirrors.
I hear a teaser on the news, "objects
not visible to the human eye," and make

a list: *unless reflected, the self's own eyes.*
*Molecules. Particles of light. The six new moons*
*of Jupiter, plus old ones.* "A downed plane,"
says the anchor, from the sky its wing

a nickel's rim in the graze of scrub
and purple thistle. Barely visible, like
the glass fish, transparent skin and spine, heart
in outline only.

The baby learns to crawl. On TV they find
a mythic giant squid with eyes the size
of dinner plates, suspended, razored tentacles
in the net, sailors agog. Everything speeds up—

*Parasites eating holes in the seawall. Mites*
*on sheets. Eyeteeth not quite cutting the gums,*
the baby learns to eat. *Contents of the stomach,*
I write. His ears fine as curls of pencil

shavings. *Fear, hunger.* Who are you?
says the voice. *Newsprint on microfiche,*
*inky thumbprint backwards and down. Unreadable,*
the baby learns bye-bye. What if you

weren't here? *The self, unless reflected.*
What if you weren't? The anchor makes a joke.
*Direction,* when the baby points—
the long arm of a crane sweeping the sky.

## Sonnet Destroyed by Crows

I was doubling
an onion against the cutting board,
My knife on the wood a wife, snap-snapping—

Something in me never

## Impasse

Snagged in the mouth of a terrible month—
even the trees, their hands
unnerving behind the frozen curtains.

Around us the dust lies
undisturbed as we whittle the winter,
the dumbness of dinner.

My mind makes my plate a circle:
The shape of what you said.
I'm thinking of snow, whether the wood

we've stacked will flare or smother.
I'm gauging the grade of our road,
the hunch that leads in one direction.

## Classifications of Languages

Those directed at the sky
Those that star and underline

Those that are cross
      Holes torn in paper, half-erased

Those that "never endeavor to advocate"

Those that confuse instructions and destructions
Those that drop objects

     All thumbs

Dead ones

Those that explain photosynthesis of phytoplankton
      in metagenomics
Those that are made up

Those that make up
Those that are enduringly dirty

Those that say how do you like them apples
      Say sorry I burned the goddamn pastry

Round-mouthed ones calling

     Those that walk, imprinting the snow

Those that lobtail
Those that lobby for the protection of the Island Marble Butterfly
      and old-world parlors

Those meaning mother
Those that lie down in the dark with a light

Those that swell
Those that whisper Salish Sea, Salish Sea

## Pulling Up the Corners

Said *you don't love me.* He was sitting
in a flannel chair, the gray behind him hardly
light. I said
        *secondhand love.*

                Circle secondhand.

B/c how could I be first?
        Not his fault I couldn't run to keep up
with myself, flying
apart—

        On my chest a ribbon bloomed.
                Italicize *honorable* for him.

        (And allow this parenthetical:

Meanwhile my watch continued
to break & we'd been waiting there how long?

Who is it he loves?
I'm not who I was.)

                Underline <u>how long love</u>.

Our breaths quickened as if in a race.

He said *don't.* It was a question. Question
the light in the room, the chair, where
        I was standing.

                Make **stand** bold,

but I wasn't. I broke down. He held
the baby, edge & center of everything.
        They seemed so far away.

                Note the distance between points.

# X

is a window sealed against
the wind. A signature or sign.

I was warned.
I climbed.

If a letter is a message, then what
is not a message? If a ladder

is a distance, then what is not a ladder?
The space between the rungs—

*this time, this time—*
hand over hand, end over

end, faster as a motor spins.
If the mind is a wheel, it burns:

sun slitting my eyes, stars
crowning. My body

hurts like a bar to the back
of the head, but so much harder.

When will it learn? If X
is unexpected, the fall is farther.

## At the Seams

Because I'm shaking my tangled head.
Because I wipe salt from the table.

As if there's a man on the corner wearing a white coat.
As if on the first day of the New Year it snows & the snow keeps
    us here.

B/c I'm shaking the salt & the tree in the window sheds its snow
    like feathers.
As if the bird in that tree is early to nest.
As if it were May.

B/c it's lucky to eat bean soup at the New Year & toss salt over
    my left shoulder.
B/c the man in the white coat waits for the light to change.

As if I raise my shoulders.
As if there's enough sun to cast my shadow with shoulders
    raised.

B/c my shoulders are raised my hands won't reach my pockets.
As if I had any extra change.
As if I had anything else to give.

As if the man in the white coat on the corner.
B/c I'm shaking.

B/c there's snow on the table & salt on the streets.
As if I meet the New Year with my shoulders raised & my
    hands up.

## What Sound Does It Make

I.

There are pieces everywhere, splinters
like the glass she shattered against the sink
just now. She keeps an eye

on the baby roaring in the corner,
practicing his lion. She keeps an eye
on the floor, diamonds

letting blood from her heel.
Prints litter the kitchen.
She gets the broom. *No*, she says. *Stay there.*

II.

Small cracks in the ceiling. If she could rest
she'd tilt her chair to watch
holes in the overturned bowl of her skull
emit their light, move
like slow-turning planets.

III.

*Would you hurt your baby?*

IV.

He's lighter when he sleeps.

The monitor's eye is red, steady, unblinking.

V.

He learns to whistle into the tea kettle's lid.
I jump at the sound of the glass in my hand slipping


VI.

My husband scrubs the floors, dishes, fixes
locks to the cabinets, gates

the stairs & doors. He fixes, fixes—
dishes, soup. I throw it up. I want

to live


VII.

*Would you hurt yourself?*


VIII.

A window is not a way out. Don't argue.
This one's wired
in a fly-swatter diamond in the door.
On the other side a man keens

*One fucking phone call PLEASE*
drawing out the plea
so they understand. They circle him.


IX.

*Would you who would you hurt
who would hurt you?*

X.

They block me in. If I could fit in the grid
of ceiling lights I'd have
a fly's eye-view:

My husband watches me. Our son
in his plush jacket. His little hood
has ears.

# Symbols to Guide Your Viewing  (II)

**Concentric circles:** ceremonial ground; or the night route repeated, see also wearing a hole in the floor;

## E:

possum tracks; a toddler's stance; shorthand for my address; adjoining rooms; can also be a bed on which three people rest, the smallest in the middle.

## Letter from Egg Lake Road

It troubles me to tell you the sky today
is the color of an unlit bulb
and that predictions call for the extinction

of Edison's incandescent.
I'll miss filaments, those fragile insects
that break when shaken, their sound

like sleet on a skylight, and the beauty
of the inner ear. I confess
wasted hours under the gooseneck lamp,

erasing. Some things
we'll never know. This house
between two trees, I can't say

how it holds me, or explain the deer
who graze outside its glass and then so surely
disappear.

## Questions for My Brother

How old are you?
> *How much time has passed?*

How do you look?
> *The same as you remember.*

Where did you go?
> *That little bit of sleep in the corners
> of your eyes.*

What are you holding?
> *A snapshot of the family.*

How long should I wait for you?
> *Check your mirror. I'm ahead.*

What will you give me?
> *My baseball mitt. My handwriting.*

What did you take with you?
> *Flavors. A red Popsicle.*

What is the sound that follows you?
> *Where did you go?*

## Hush

I lie and say there are no ghosts.
Near our bed, hair magnetized, shock
on blanket and pajamas

I could pat him, turn him toward the door,
but he has *owl, moon, hoot*—and just then a train

loans its lonely sound to the static
of our neighborhood. And that sound
like sand is everywhere. We've tried

to show him the world straight up,
from carrots pulled
to the crow at the peak of the roof.

Our present fresh as paint. He loves
our lies: *Horses have hands. Houses*

*have footprints*— New floors
over old. Walls punched in, sockets moved,
hidden wires. He doesn't know.

He found *ghost* and shook it loose.
It has him, and it's his.

## Maps of Childhood

I already know the route there
and back there and
back like a weary animal
in the dark. On long car trips
I was told to count telephone poles.
Memory is not one thing but
I prefer to keep the mountains
on my left.

## And None of Mine Own

When I went, I went west
until there was no more. Forsook
the eastern cities and seaboard, shied the lights

for stars. I addressed my west as darling.
West is a boy with a bucket

of beach on his arm: won't dress
for dinner or come when he's called.

Won't listen. Wears antlers.
I asked my west how best to hold him
but lost his answer

among the rocks he skipped across the lake.
My west is a narrow stretch

longed for. He whittles trees
to teeth and feeds them to a bone-filled fire.
I followed him like a trail

but oh my west is merciless, a boy
who leaves as I left with light on his back,
an arrow of grief in his heel.

## Questions for My Brother

How long should I wait for you?
> *You're always just rising from the table*
> *after I've found my coat and gone.*

Where did you go?
> *Remember our front porch?*
> *The sprinkler's turning arc, our hands*
> *and faces pressed against the screen?*

What did you take with you?
> *You saw me leaving.*

How old are you?
> *Eleven.*

What are you holding?
> *Nothing. My hands are crossed.*

What is the sound that follows you?
> *You?*

What will you give me?
> *A glimpse.*

How do you look?
> *Check your mirror: The motion of your hand*
> *brushing past your ear.*

## Black Forest

All winter I've stared. This window is winter
 *Dear___, no phone since we left*
& reads like a block of ice, like vision
 *almost a month ago. This morning*
without my coke-bottles on.
 *I bundled the baby & walked fast.*
It shares the dark & my superstitions: three witches,
 *My mouth went numb*
a draft. I moved the bassinet. If this window
 *from cold, my glasses fogged—*
is a mind it marbles with the late afternoon
 *I turned back. Tired of*
light. From outside, a small room lined
 *my own voice. Everything*
with the radiators' teeth. If this window
 *I say I say twice. Did I tell you*
is a mirror it's a reasonable facsimile
 *he looks like Shawn? Maybe a shadow of*
of me, a little fatter, blurred
 *my brother in him. Why is it*
recall. If it's a door to my past, it's cracked
 *death is never done? You said*
just so the blind clatters when I ask
 *I cannot shut the door. It's true*
who's there. This window is my baby,
 *his birth made me afraid.*
all eyes. Its portrait of the trees shows
 *Nothing here*
each bare joint as wishbone. If this window
 *could harm him. Farmland, horses*
is my body you must see
 *serene, the sky intact. A few people,*
its borders. How far can it travel?
 *their dogs. If only my mind weren't so wild.*

## Topography

The little mound of childhood
at the top of the map:
My brother died.

I dialed circles in the dirt
around it. Satellite,
my red sneakers,
my one long vowel amplified.

## Alone at the Edge of the Painting

I like a landscape to myself
where the green light
is a just-brushed field
of hair. Flowers tip

their noses:
The light won't last.
In the distance the clouds are clay

and the trees rumble. My horses
hide behind them
wearing imaginary coats.
They won't be nudged

no matter how I call them,
softly like this
*come out come out*
or with my voice raised—

Your hair must still be blond.
I'm older than our mother
and I lug our mother's fear
on my hip and with my arms.

Show yourself. I'm tired.
The grass is an address: yes
I'd like to stay
and lie down—

In the crowded trees
leaves shuffle but there's no sound.
No birds, and the flowers still

stupidly expectant.
The grass has so many pockets.
It's about to rain.
It won't.

## Questions for My Brother

Where did you go?
>               *you? A hallway. I'm ahead.*

How do you look?
>                               *our hands*
>               *and faces pressed against the screen?*
>               *in the corners of your eyes. My hands*

What will you give me?
>                       *Flavors. your mirror.*
>                       *You saw me leaving.*

What did you take with you?
>               *of the family. just rising from the table*
>                       *A glimpse.*

What are you holding?
>                       *My baseball mitt.*
>               *your favorite book. I've found my coat*

How old are you?
>               *A snapshot A red Popsicle. Check*
>                       *My handwriting*

What is the sound that follows you?
>                       *your hand*
>                 *brushing past your ear.*
>               *The sprinkler's turning arc,*

How long should I wait for you?
>                 *How much time has passed?*
>                 *The same as you remember.*

## The Day After Yesterday

So much has yet to be invented.
We're practicing how to fold our boats.
He wonders what the sea was like
before color while I return again and again
to the same cabinet for a memory.
The cry of the hinge
makes me forget which one.
I like how the mirrored door shows
the trees over my shoulder
as a painting of themselves. Behind them
chimneys unmoored. He wants a lake.
As I was saying, we believe
birds derived from the color blue.

# Symbols to Guide Your Viewing  (III)

**U** **shapes:**
a person raising her hands to show
puzzlement, as in, what now; eggs in
the hammock of her apron, or a wet
load of laundry;   depending on
position may indicate a welcome;
depending on position may indicate a
frown.

**Arcs:**
windbreaks; a rare halo; the theory
that what goes up must come down;
also the status of a character as it
unfolds throughout the story; see
also ball in mid-air.

## This & Thus Far

*I think I'm all right again,*
I said, after two glasses

of red & dinner on its way.
We were sitting by the kitchen

in Italy, our baby tucked in
for the night. He was three months.

He was three. We were in Italy
& France. In a restaurant

a castle/ forest or/ farmhouse.
There was a church

at the bottom of the hill
& cats. A quince tree

a rake. He was thirteen moons.
Beetles' shells cracked

under his feet.
He was so new. He slept.

When he didn't sleep I cried.
It was August-Christmas-

early March. We'd seen
our share. I slipped

in my seat, my napkin
loose in my lap. His new word

was *bird.* My mind
had wandered.

My husband raised his glass.
I pressed my eyes in place.

We left Rome burning
Paris buried in the snow.

## The Winter He Is One

Near the stables
a trough

An iron bathtub
iced—

Like a horse he had to
break me

his hand the star
between

my lowered
eyes

my lowered
eyes lord

& bring me back
broken

Here the fence
There the field

# Photographs of Birds, Featuring Their Understudies

*They have to function according to their character:*
  *they are obliged to migrate,*
*to follow the natural force to move. –Jean Luc Mylayne*


Heart overhead. Heart against a vast blue sky.
Heart in a barn, observing a cat.
Heart with a hay cart.
Heart on pillar and post.
Heart riffling red leaves.
Plate 12. Heart, 1980.
Heart with school bus approaching.
Heart at the window.
Heart with a moth in its mouth.
Back view of a heart.
Heart camouflaged. Dark-eyed heart.
Heart in scrubby landscape.
Heart with horses. Skittish heart.
Heart beside red and black stitched boots.
Heart near a blue truck.
Beautiful blue-crested heart.
Startled heart. Heart with cactus bloom.
Heart on one leg, heart on a wire.
Plate 67. 2000. Heart feeding heart's young.
Open-beaked heart, head feathers askew.

## And Then

In the windows we were drawn:
I held my knobby baby
in dawn's automotive light.
A fleet of cars sailed by
as school-kids stomped their boots
shook their shiny coats.
I put my baby in a basket.
We slept in fits & as the weather
turned we started to grow older.

I bounced him *hobbledy-hoy, hobbledy-hoy!*
I wound my wobbly bumpkin
& in the garden
let him go. We went in circles.
*This is the way the farmers ride.*
Another year. Another.
I lost count of worn-out shoes.
Bees came to the flowers of his ears.
His hair got long.

Around us
red leaves lettered to the ground
& I became a tree.
I swung my boy like a bell
by his knees. His mouth
made the shape of a song.
Where had he heard it?
I listened to the tune.
This was not a song I'd known.

## Prehistory

I roam the slope of the living room floor.
Marbles, boulders, roll southwest
& collect in the corner. The seas

have retreated. I'm footsore:
stegosaurus plates in one instep, the snapped
ribs of a T-rex under my left heel.

The boy responsible digs
in a box of dirt, wearing goggles
& primly brushing bones. Polite,

the scientist declines
my roars. He works out on the porch,
his hammer & chisel ringing
like a windy flag against its pole.

## Invocation

O potato, freckled-in-rows-of-four-where-forked
Heart, so dogged, so dog-like, bumping & literal,
And the brain who thinks it's better, my scheming
Separatist brain, my hoarder, hunched accordionist
How I've hated you, no less & no more than
My automatic lungs—wait, now, wait, now—
Hate the mouth asking *How many times have I told you?*
*What language am I speaking?* Shut up. Curse you:
I repeat, & this skin I shed but am not rid of, to this shaped
Rubber glove skin, a curse. A curse on the hands
Which had not & wanted, which had & did not want.
Curse my arms: I have flung him. I have held him down.
Curse my fingers: button-pushers, bruisers, crooks.
Curse the good ear who listened when the voice insisted
*What kind of mother? Are you?* –O, but bless
The deaf one, who scans for signs & still responds
To touch, to shadows that align like birds above the water.
Bless my arms: I gather him. Bless my hands, their strokes.
Bless the legs who kick to save themselves, & all right yes
This whole damned lot—gristle, tongue & stuffing, fat
Balloons, the eyes' horizon—& god help you,
Bless you, unlovely thudding pump, who sinks & sinks
And bobs back up

# Cuttings

Nights in my head
I make lists such as
things lost:

sunhat, stroller (stolen),
little wooden train

or tied together:
font, fountain
fontanel

While our son's helix
spins against

our straightened lines—
feet to ribs
to spines & chins

I think of rejoinders
his demands

to be picked up
How I carry the branch of him

grafted but
he leans away saying
Hold me better.

## Spoke

For every language, a landscape: park
your car there, one says. One is an alpine lake

& your thin skin, cold traveling your bones
like a bell. One, cracks in a palace wall, one cobblestones,

here smoke, a cord of wood, one a crowded train
flagging at the tenements, clothes lining

the sky red. Another is a bowl
of horse flesh, a fish you must eat whole,

eyes, cheeks, some beer to wash it down,
you the honored guest. A furrowed brow

should you refuse. Some are locked gates.
Some offer all they have when you recite

hopefully *thank you, good afternoon, please, where is. . .?*
One is the wrong shoes. One holds up its fists

as if to fight. Head of a man, frieze of lions, all
museums of your wordlessness. In these hollows

you filled yourself, rooting to one world: your year-old
mouth made apple, a line of trees, its alphabet of crows.

## Sweet Pea Preschool of the Arts

Only a handful of hours, & you
slow, stalled at breakfast.
Where are your shoes, your coat?
I want you to go.
Sewn to me,

your smile
ravels when I let the teacher
have you. For a moment I'm stuck,
then weirdly light.

What are you, spider?
You appear
in a hat with eight legs,
carrying a note: *Today I was good at* <u>art</u>.
*My mood today was* <u>happy</u>.
You use glitter

to describe everything, bring us
fevers, croup,
decoupage. Trees
in your "Winter Collage
No. 2" march off the skyline.
Our days fill

with laundry, snot,
shower steam. Barking. I remove
the glue, take you back

& back again. Good at
<u>circle time</u>, <u>yoga</u>, <u>French</u>—
You learn to say excuse me,
raise your hand, wear

a paper crown. I'm not a traitor.
I want you there
& here. Come home now

come home
in a red feathered mask
for the New Year. I made you go.

## Godzilla Movie

spring flurries
and a boy
in monster boots
stamps grass

crocuses
peek
up

## Fable

I make a list of wishes then cross them out.
Listen instead to mice transcribing
numbers in the wall by my head
as I try to sleep under a grave
skylight, under trees. The frogs hold forth

their deep belief; crickets treble;
this is followed by a short assembly
of silence. Stranded, my nightgown covered
in vines, my dreams a disturbance with legs—
It's taken me this long to become human.

## Praise the Present Tense

& the invisible boy who hides, hands over his eyes, in the center
 of the room.
Praise evidence: mouth prints on windows,
his tongue's snail on the long glass doors
I've told him not to lick.
Praise the cup that breaks because
I've told him not to break it.
Praise socks in the hallway, socks in every corner
& two shoes flung in four directions.
Praise scattershot pocks on walls, the damn toy hammer that
 made them.
Praise spackle & paint.
Praise the balloon losing air & tulips floating, open as baskets.
Praise an aerial view, the partly clearing day.
Glory to what's small & undone.
Bless him & keep him where he stands,
with me seeking, pretending not to see.

## Story

A sunspot, at first a floating dart, it grew
a pair of ears. In water
it replaced the water until it filled the jar.

It was my diminishment.
It smiled like a melon. I lived
on the doughnut rungs

of my wrists. Too soon
too big for its britches, I take that tone
& jab up, waving my arms.

I fly from side streets
scaring pigeons & scooters.
I never sleep

or else only sleep with my feet on its back.
There are holes
in my alphabet, I can't remember

the numbers between 12 & 16
but I'm working
on the question of God.

Meanwhile, it hates cheese. I won't eat.
When it shows my teeth, I worry.
I worry: too much,

not enough? When it clatters, I start to fall apart.
Set it on a stool with a spoon & a pot.
Let it ring. Let me let me.

## Mouth

He sang *orchid* &
it opened
yellow lion-headed

dare

I warned him but
he laughed
*what teeth*

put his fingertip
just

　　　there

## Outpost

Like a truck in mud my escape
was nothing fancy, no glissando—
it was years of walking funny under
the weight of a piano until I bought
a truck. I refused to let the flat sky
sink me. I backed up over and over
until the photo I was in had to let me go.
Check out those onlookers gawking, frozen,
their coats too small. Irritated
by my mess, my strange insistent beeping,
they think they know better, think
who does she think she is? Me in the corner
trying to swing this rig around.

## Boy in Red Shorts

Because there's no snow my son lies down in sand
to make his angel. Sometimes

he is human: how surprised I am to find
his mouth

swearing *Jesus!*
    when he bumps his head, *dammit!*

when he tries to reach the tap. It's almost
funny. What does he know

about angels?
I dig my feet into the dents he's made,

his print, arms fanned—
he who crushes cars, he who dinosaurs
& pirates—

Now a kite unwinds a kind of window.
Beach grass leans. When he stands I shake him out

& keep him.

## Anniversary

You're the icing. I'm the swarm of candles
on my cake. It's my birthday. Bring me an island.

I'm like an atlas: Impossible to find Delaware.
Beware my small moods. Beware.

I cover my eyes. I know what's coming.
Don't look. Will you look at what's coming?

Around the bend. Some wilderness I part
with a jackknife dive. You on the banks in the dark.

Your voice weaves through my five belt loops.
Air changes angles when you haul me up.

As angels dangle from pulleys in a play:
Something hovers over us, always.

I replace the roof shingle by shingle.
You keep rain off, tap gutters when they're full.

There's too much. There's not enough.
You say, just the right amount in every bowl & cup.

Bad at math, I'm dumb as a bell, clumsy.
But rapt. On the tag mark X & X. And O for me.

## Susurrus

The grass grows under and stumbles us
in its variety: this kind long, this salty
and this a cowlick or curled

mimic of the black snake. This lies,
this waves, this threatens the Snowy Plover
and this presses us with burrs.

So slowly the birds don't know.
The cane chair at the bay's edge is innocent,
and the flagstone path.

On purpose I was lost in a field like this.
By which I measure distance now,

the last light cresting. Only his shoulders.
Only the top of his head shows.

I used to think returning
was the same as never going forward.

The grass agrees to gather us.
It allows asters and the logs the tides bring
to rest. Things I meant to say

will have to stay meant.
Our boy cuts in, clutching a feather.

# Notes

"Symbols to Guide Your Viewing" took suggestions from museum placards accompanying a 2012 exhibit, "Ancestral Modern: Australian Aboriginal Art," at Seattle Art Museum.

"Wearing the Terrarium" happened after I stuck my head in "Biosphere Built for Two," an art installation by Vaughn Bell.

"Sonnet Destroyed by Crows" and all of its ghosts are for Kary.

Linda Gregg's poem "Stuff" and its directives guided "Pulling Up the Corners."

"Questions for My Brother" is after Mark Strand's "Elegy for My Father."

Jean Luc Mylayne has been photographing birds for more than 30 years. "Photographs of Birds, Featuring Their Understudies" are captions I created in response to photos in his self-titled book.

"And None of Mine Own" owes its title to the lyrics of the traditional cowboy ballad "Git Along Little Dogies."

"Alone at the Edge of a Painting" was inspired by Hans Thoma's painting "Calm Before the Storm," and two lines from Walt Whitman's "Song of Myself": "Or I guess the grass is itself a child. . ." and "And now it seems to me the beautiful uncut hair of graves."

# Acknowledgements

My sincere thanks to the editors of the magazines and journals in which these poems first appeared, sometimes in slightly different versions:

*Bateau:* "Prehistory"
*Beloit Poetry Journal:* "The Winter He Is One," "Boy in Red Shorts," "Lament for Seven Minus Some," "Suspect," "Directions," "Story," "Praise the Present Tense"
*Crab Creek Review:* "Alone at the Edge of the Painting," "Maps of Childhood"
*Dark Sky Question:* "Sonnet Destroyed By Crows"
*Diagram:* "Pulling Up the Corners"
*Field*: "Hush," "Letter from Egg Lake Road"
*Filter:* "Questions for My Brother"
*The Laurel Review:* "Mouth," "Anniversary," "This & Thus Far"
*The Monarch Review:* "Impasse," "Photographs of Birds, Featuring Their Understudies"
*New Orleans Review:* "Spoke"
*Poetry Northwest:* "Fable," "Susurrus," "The Day After Yesterday"
*Pontoon Eight: An Anthology of Washington State Poets:* "What Sound Does It Make"
*Pool:* "Invocation"
*Rattapallax:* "Classifications of Languages," "Wearing the Terrarium"
*Rhino:* "At the Seams"
*Seattle Magazine:* "And None of Mine Own"
*Snakeskin Poetry Webzine:* "Sweet Pea Preschool of the Arts"
*West Branch:* "Objects Not Visible to the Human Eye"

"Directions," "Anniversary," and "Spoke" were featured on *Verse Daily.* "Invocation" and "This & Thus Far" were reprinted in *Pontoon Nine: An Anthology of Washington State Poets* (Floating Bridge Press, 2006); "Sweet Pea Preschool of the Arts" in *Pontoon Ten* (2008). "Invocation," "And None of Mine Own," and "Classifications of Languages" are included in *Fire On Her Tongue: An eBook Anthology of Contemporary Women's Poetry* (Two Sylvias Press, 2012).

Many of these poems were collected in a chapbook, *What Sound Does It Make,* winner of the 2007 Concrete Wolf Poetry Award.

My thanks also goes to Washington State Artist Trust and King County 4Culture, for grants that supported the writing of some of these poems, and to the Helen Riaboff Whiteley Center for invaluable time and space in which to work.

So many people helped me in the years it took to shape this book that any list is incomplete. For their insight and encouragement I'm grateful to my friends, teachers, and co-conspirators all along the way, including Linda Bierds, Shannon Borg, Kathleen Flenniken, Anna Maria Hong, Rebecca Hoogs, Kasey Langley, Becka McKay, Jennifer Preisman, Martha Silano, Megan Snyder-Camp, and Kary Wayson. I also want to send out three cheers to Eric Zener for generous permission to use his painting on the cover, and to Tebot Bach Press and Ralph Angel for giving this book a home.

Thanks to Patrick, Lois, and Ryan Malone, for the stories and for believing; and finally, to Shawn and Peter Wong— you're where the world and words settle down.

**TEBOT BACH**
A 501(c) (3) Literary Arts Education Non Profit

**THE TEBOT BACH MISSION:** advancing literacy, strengthening community, and transforming life experience with the power of poetry through readings, workshops, and publications.

**THE TEBOT BACH PROGRAMS**

1. A poetry reading and writing workshop series for venues such as homeless shelters, battered women's shelters, nursing homes, senior citizen daycare centers, Veterans organizations, hospitals, AIDS hospices, correctional facilities which serve under represented populations. Participating poets include: John Balaban, Brendan Constantine, Megan Doherty, Richard Jones, Dorianne Laux, M.L. Leibler, Lawrence Lieberman, Carol Topal, Cecilia Woloch.

2. A poetry reading and writing workshop series for the community Southern California at large, and for schools K-University. The workshops feature local, national, and international teaching poets. Participating poets include: David St. John, Charles Webb, Wanda Coleman, Amy Gerstler, Patricia Smith, Holly Prado, Dorothy Barresi, W.D. Ehrhart, Tom Lux, Rebecca Seiferle, Suzanne Lummis, Michael Datcher, B.H. Fairchild, Cecilia Woloch, Chris Abani, Laurel Ann Bogen, Sam Hamill, David Lehman, Christopher Buckley, Mark Doty.

3. A publishing component to give local, national, and international poets a venue for publishing and distribution.

Tebot Bach
Box 7887
Huntington Beach, CA 92615-7887
714-968-0905
www.tebotbach.org